CONTENTS

PYTHON CERTIFICATION EXAM

PCAP-31-03 – Complete Preparation

Latest Practice Tests

Are you preparing for the Python Certification Exam PCAP-31-03?

Look no further for an **exclusive preparation resource** designed to **help** you **ace** the **exam** on your **first try.**

Save both your time and money with this newly released book.

This **comprehensive book** offers a **unique opportunity** to **assess your knowledge** and **practice** with **real exam questions**. It's **packed** with **the most up-to-date questions, detailed explanations**, and **valuable references**.

Our new book covers all the essential **topics** included in the Python Certification **PCAP-31-03 exam**. It's **strategically designed** to **boost** your **confidence, ensuring** that **you're well-prepared** to take on the **actual exam** by **testing** your **knowledge** and **skills** across all the **required subject areas**.

To **pass** the **Python Certification Exam PCAP-31-03 on your initial attempt**, it's crucial to **invest** your **efforts in mastering** these **PCAP-31-03 questions**, which **provide the latest insights** into the **entire exam syllabus.**

Official exam details:

Total questions in the PCAP-31-03 real exam: **40**

Time allocated for answering these questions: **65 minutes**

Passing score: 70%

Earning a PCAP certification can **significantly enhance your career prospects**.

Python, **being** the **programming language with the broadest array of opportunities**, offers **limitless possibilities** in the **21st Century**.

As **your proficiency in Python deepens**, your **potential career** paths **expand** across various industries and job roles.

The **PCAP certification serves** as a valuable **qualification** for those **seeking to gain the fundamental skills** and **expertise** required to **progress** towards more **advanced** and **specialized roles** in **fields** like Software **Development, Security, Networking, IoT**, and **engineering**, which often come with **higher earning potential.**

Welcome!

PRACTICE TEST I

1) At the end of the while loop, what will be the value of the 'i' variable?

```
i=0
while i ! =0:
        i=i-1
else:
        i=i+1
```

A. 1

B. 0

C. 2

D. The variable becomes unavailable

2) Which operators are used for performing bitwise shifts? (Choose two.)

A. --

B. ++

C. <<

D. >>

3) Upon completion of the following loop, what will be the value of the 'i' variable?

```
for i in range (10):
    pass
```

A. 10

B. The variable becomes unavailable

C. 11

D. 9

4) 1+-2

Regarding the given expression, determine:

A. It is equal to 1

B. It is invalid

C. It is equal to 2

D. It is equal to -1

5) What are the primary functions of a compiler? (Choose two.)

A. Rearrange the source code to improve clarity

B. Verify the correctness of the source code

C. Execute the source code

D. Translate the source code into machine code

6) What will be the result of the provided code?

```
a= 'ant'
b= "bat"
c= 'camel'
print (a, b, c, sep= '''')
```

A. ant' bat' camel

B. ant"bat" camel

C. antbatcamel

D. print (a, b, c, sep= '" ')

7) What is the anticipated output of the following code snippet?

```
i=5
while i>0:
        i=i //2
        if i % 2=0:
                break
    else:
            i+=1
print (i)
```

A. The code contains errors

B. 3

C. 7

D. 15

8) How many lines does the subsequent code snippet produce?

```
for i in range (1, 3):
    print ("*", end= "")
else:
    print ("*")
```

A. Three

B. One

C. Two

D. Four

9) Which of the following literals represents the value 34.23? (Choose two.)

A. .3423e2

B. 3423e-2

C. .3423e-2

D. 3423e2

10) What is the expected output of the following code snippet?

```
a=2
if a>0:
    a+=1
else:
    a-=1
print(a)
```

A. 3

B. 1

C. 2

D. The code is erroneous

11) Assuming that the following snippet has been successfully executed, which of the equations are True? (Choose two.)

```
a= [1]
b=a
a[0] = 0
```

A. len(a) == len (b)

B. b [0] +1 ==a [0]

C. a [0] == b [0]

D. a [0] + 1 ==b [0]

12) Assuming that the following snippet has been successfully executed, which of the equations are False? (Choose two.)

$$a=[0]$$
$$b=a \ [:]$$
$$a[0]=1$$

A. len(a)== len (b)

B. a [0]-1 ==b [0]

C. a [0]== b [0]

D. b [0] - 1 ==a [0]

13) Which of the following statements are true about Python strings? (Choose two.)

A. Python strings are equivalent to lists.

B. Python strings support concatenation.

C. Python strings can be sliced like lists.

D. Python strings are mutable.

14) Which of the following statements are true regarding lists and tuples in Python? (Choose two.)

A. Lists cannot be included in tuples.

B. Tuples can be included in lists.

C. Tuples cannot be included in tuples.

D. Lists can be included in lists.

15) Assuming that a string is six or more letters long, the slice [1:-2] of the string is shorter than the original string by:

A. Four characters

B. Three characters

C. One character

D. Two characters

16) What is the expected output of the following snippet?

```
lst = [1,2,3,4]
lst = lst [-3:-2]
lst= lst[-1]
print (lst)
```

A. 1

B. 4

C. 2

D. 3

17) What is the expected output of the following snippet?

```
s= 'abc'
for i in len(s):
    s[i] = s[i].upper ( )
print(s)
```

A. abc

B. The code will cause a runtime exception

C. ABC

D. 123

18) How many elements will the list2 list contain after execution of the following snippet?

```
list1 = [False for i in range (1, 10) ]
list2 = list1 [-1:1:-1]
```

A. zero

B. five

C. seven

D. three

19) What would you used instead of XXX if you want to check weather a certain 'key' exists in a dictionary called dict? (Choose two.)

if XXX:
    print   Key exists

A. 'key' in dict

B. dict ['key'] != None

C. dict.exists ('key')

D. 'key' in dict.keys ( )

20) You need data which can act as a simple telephone directory. You can obtain it with the following clauses (Choose two.) (assume that no other items have been created before)

A. dir={'Mom': 5551234567, 'Dad': 5557654321}

B. dir= {'Mom': '5551234567', 'Dad': '5557654321'}

C. dir= {Mom: 5551234567, Dad: 5557654321}

D. dir= {Mom: '5551234567', Dad: '5557654321'}

21) How can a Python module behave when it is executed or imported?

A. It can differentiate its behavior between execution and import.

B. Its behavior depends on the Python version.

C. It can run like regular code but cannot differentiate its behavior between execution and import.

D. It is not possible for a module to run; it can only be imported.

22) Select the valid fun () invocations:

```
def fun (a, b=0):
    return a*b
```

(Choose two.)

A. fun (b=1)

B. fun (a=0)

C. fun (b=1, 0)

D. fun (1)

23) What information can be inferred from a file name like "services, cpython 36.pyc"?

(Choose three.)

A. The interpreter used to generate the file is version 3.6.

B. It has been produced by CPython.

C. It is the 36th version of the file.

D. The file comes from the "services.py" source file.

24) What is the expected behavior of the following snippet?
It will:

$$\text{def a (l, I) :}$$
$$\text{return l [I]}$$

$$\text{print (a (0, [1]))}$$

A. cause a runtime exception

B. print 1

C. print 0, [1]

D. print [1]

25) How can you simplify a long package path like the one below?

import alpha .beta . gamma .delta .epsilon .zeta

A. You can make an alias for the name using the alias keyword.

B. There's nothing you can do; you need to accept it.

C. You can shorten it to "alpha.zeta," and Python will find the proper connection.

D. You can make an alias for the name using the as keyword.

26) What will be the output of the following code?

```
str = 'abcdef'
def fun (s) :
    del s [2]
    return s


print (fun (str) )
```

A. "abcef"

B. The program will result in a runtime exception or error.

C. "acdef"

D. "abdef"

27) What is the expected output of the following code?

```
def f (n) :
    if n == 1:
        return '1'
    return str (n) + f (n-1)


print (f (2) )
```

A. 21

B. 2

C. 3

D. 12

28) What is the expected outcome of the following code snippet?

```
def x( ) :          # line 01
    return 2        # line 02

x= 1 + x ( )        # line 03
print (x)           # line 04
```

It will:

A. Cause a runtime exception on line 02.

B. Cause a runtime exception on line 01.

C. Cause a runtime exception on line 03.

D. Print "3."

29) What is the expected behavior of the following code?

```
def f (n):
        for i in range (1, n+1) :
            yield I


print (f(2) )
```

A. It will print "4321."

B. It will print "<generator object f at (some hex digits)."

C. It will cause a runtime exception.

D. It will print "1234."

30) If you need a function that does nothing, what would you use instead of XXX?

def idler ( ):
XXX

(Choose two.)

A. pass

B. return

C. exit

D. None

31) Is it possible to safely check if a class/object has a certain attribute?

A. Yes, by using the hasattr attribute.

B. Yes, by using the hasattr() method.

C. Yes, by using the hassattr() function.

D. No, it is not possible.

32) The first parameter of each method:

A. Holds a reference to the currently processed object.

B. Is always set to None.

C. Is set to a unique random value.

D. Is set by the first argument's value.

33) What is the simplest possible class definition in Python?

A. class X:

B. class X: pass

C. class X: return

D. class X: { }

34) How can you access an exception object's components and store them in an object called e in Python?

A. except Exception (e) :

B. except e= Exception :

C. except Exception as e:

D. Such an action is not possible in Python.

35) What is a variable stored separately in every object called?

A. There are no such variables; all variables are shared among objects.

B. A class variable.

C. An object variable.

D. An instance variable.

36) You have a writable stream named "s." How do you write a line to the stream?

A. s.write("Hello\n")

B. write(s, "Hello")

C. s.writeln("Hello")

D. s.writeline("Hello")

37) You need to read just one character from a stream named "s." Which statement would you use?

A. ch = read(s, 1)

B. ch = s.input(1)

C. ch = input(s, 1)

D. ch = s.read(1)

38) What can you deduce from the following statement? (Choose two.)

str = open("file.txt", "rt")

A. str is a string read in from the file named "file.txt."

B. A newline character translation will be performed during the reads.

C. If "file.txt" does not exist, it will be created.

D. The opened file cannot be written with the use of the str variable.

39) The following class hierarchy is given. What is the expected output of the code?

```python
class A:
    def a (self) :
        print ("A", end= ' ')
    def b (self) :
        self.a ( )

class B (A):
    def a (self) :
        print ("B", end= ' ')
    def do (self):
        self.b ( )

class C (A):
    def a (self):
        print ("C", end= ' ')
    def do (self):
        self.b ( )

B ( ) . do ( )
C ( ) . do ( )
```

A. BB

B. CC

C. AA

D. BC

40) Python's built-in function named open() tries to open a file and returns:

A. An integer value identifying an opened file.

B. An error code (0 means success).

C. A stream object.

D. Always None.

ANSWERS AND EXPLANATION

1) The correct answer is A. 1.

In the given code, the 'while' loop condition is "i != 0," and the initial value of 'i' is 0. Since the loop condition is not met initially, the loop doesn't execute, and the 'else' block is executed, which increments 'i' by 1. Therefore, at the end of the loop, the value of 'i' is 1.

Initially i value is 0, while condition fails as not equal to 0 So, it enters into else block and execute the increment statement. Now i become 1

2) Correct answer: CD

C. << (Left Shift Operator):

The "<<" operator is used for left-shifting bits in a binary number.

It moves the bits to the left, effectively multiplying the number by 2 raised to the specified power.

For example, if you have the binary number 0010 (which represents 2 in decimal), left-shifting it by one position becomes 0100 (which represents 4 in decimal).

D. >> (Right Shift Operator):

The ">>" operator is used for right-shifting bits in a binary number.

It moves the bits to the right, effectively dividing the number by 2 raised to the specified power.

For example, if you have the binary number 0100 (which represents 4 in decimal), right-shifting it by one position becomes 0010 (which represents 2 in decimal).

These operators are commonly used in programming to manipulate individual bits within binary numbers, which can be useful in various applications, including low-level operations and optimizations.

x = 8   # 8 in Binary: 1000

y = x >> 2   # Right shift by 2 positions: 0010 (in binary) which is 2 in decimal

print(y)   # Output: 2

x = 4   # 4 in Binary: 0100

y = x << 2   # Left shift by 2 positions: 10000 (in binary) which is 16 in decimal

print(y)   # Output: 16

Reference:

https://www.geeksforgeeks.org/basic-operators-python/

3) The correct answer is:

D. 9

9 is the Answer. Pass only means there are no statements to

execute it does not mean the variable is unavailable. Try a Print statement Print(i) after the For Loop and there is your result.

Just try to print the value of i after the loop, you would get 9 as result.

```
<code>
for i in range(10):
    pass
print(i)
</code>
```

In a 'for' loop using range(10), 'i' will iterate through the values from 0 to 9 (inclusive). So, at the end of the loop, the value of 'i' will be 9, not 10.

4) Regarding the expression "1+-2," it is equal to:

D. It is equal to -1

The plus sign followed by a negative number is equivalent to subtraction, so 1 - 2 results in -1.

Mathematically, the expression can be thought of as:

$1+(-2)$

When you add a negative number, it's the same as subtracting its absolute value. So the above expression becomes:

$1-2$

Which equals -1.

Therefore, the output of 1+-2 is -1.

5) Correct answer: BD

B. Verify the correctness of the source code

D. Translate the source code into machine code

Explanation:

A compiler primarily checks the source code for correctness and translates it into machine code for execution. It does not typically rearrange the source code for clarity, and it is not responsible for executing the code itself.

6) Correct answer: B

In the provided code:

a = 'ant'

b = "bat"

c = 'camel'

print(a, b, c, sep="")

The print function is used to display the values of variables a, b, and c, separated by the double quotation mark " (as specified by sep=""). This means that the values of the variables will be printed with double quotation marks between them.

So, the output will be: "ant"bat" camel"

7) Correct answer: A

Inside the if for comparing the result of the modulus must be if i % 2 == 0:

The code does indeed contain errors due to the incorrect use of the assignment operator = in the if condition. The correct code should be:

i = 5

```
while i > 0:
    i = i // 2
    if i % 2 == 0:
        break
    else:
        i += 1
print(i)
```

With this correction, the code will work as expected, and the output is 2. So, option A, "The code contains errors," is the accurate choice for the original code you provided.

8) Correct answer: B

The provided code contains a syntax error. The use of the "else" statement after the "for" loop is not valid in Python. A loop should not have an "else" block directly after it. Therefore, the code cannot produce any output.

So, the correct answer is:

B. One

The code generates one line of output, which is "*".

9) Correct answer: AB

A. .3423e2:

This represents 34.23 in scientific notation. The "e2" part means multiplying the number before it by 10 to the power of 2, which is 100. So, .3423e2 is equal to 34.23.

B. 3423e-2:

This also represents 34.23 in scientific notation. The "e-2" part means dividing the number before it by 10 to the power of -2, which is 1/100. So, 3423e-2 is equal to 34.23.

Both of these notations correctly represent the value 34.23 using scientific notation, which is a common way to express large or small numbers in a compact form.

For representing decimal values both A and B must be written.

10) Correct answer: D

The code snippet you provided has a syntax issue. The correct way to write an if statement in Python is to use a colon (:) to indicate the start of the block for each condition. Here's the corrected version of the code:

a = 2

if a > 0:

    a += 1

else:

    a -= 1

print(a)

Now, with this corrected code, the expected output will be:

A. 3

The code will increment the value of a by 1 because a is initially 2, which is greater than 0, so the if block is executed, and a is increased by 1. The final value of a is 3, which is printed.

11) Correct answer: AC

Let's analyze the given code snippet first:

a = [1]

b = a

a[0] = 0

In this snippet, a is assigned a list [1], and then b is assigned the reference to the same list that a is referencing. So, a and b both refer to the same list in memory. When you modify the list through one variable, it will affect the other variable as well.

Now, let's evaluate the equations:

A. len(a) == len(b) - True (Both a and b reference the same list, and the length of the list is still 1, so this is True.)

B. b[0] + 1 == a[0] - False (After the assignment a[0] = 0, a[0] becomes 0, and b[0] is also 0 since they both reference the same list. So, 0 + 1 is not equal to 0, making this False.)

C. a[0] == b[0] - True (Both a and b reference the same list, and a[0] and b[0] are both 0, so this is True.)

D. a[0] + 1 == b[0] - False (As mentioned earlier, a[0] and b[0] are both 0, so 0 + 1 is not equal to 0, making this False.)

So, the correct options are A and C.

For you who thought it was AD, here is the explanation:

When you have an array in a variable and set it to another variable, they share the same id, that means they point to the same array.

a = [1]

b = a

print(id(a), id(b)) # same id

Since a==b, when you set a[0] = 0, you are "also" doing b[0] = 0

12) Correct answer: CD

C. a [0]== b [0]

D. b [0] - 1 ==a [0]

As the question says which equations are False

a = [0]

b = a[:]

a[0] = 1

a[0] # is 1

b[0] # is 0

so:

print(len(a) == len(b)) # => True

print(a[0] - 1 == b[0]) # => True

print(a[0] == b[0]) # => False

print(b[0] - 1 == a[0]) # => False

13) The correct answers are:

B. Python strings support concatenation.

C. Python strings can be sliced like lists.

B. Python strings support concatenation:

Python strings can be concatenated using the + operator. This means you can combine two or more strings together to create a new string. For example, "Hello, " + "World" results in the string "Hello, World."

C. Python strings can be sliced like lists:

Python strings can be sliced using slice notation, similar to lists. You can access a portion of a string by specifying the start and end indices within square brackets, like my_string[start:end]. This allows you to extract substrings or specific parts of a string.

The other options are not true:

A. Python strings are not equivalent to lists. Strings and lists are different data types in Python.

D. Python strings are immutable, meaning you cannot change the characters in a string directly. You can create a new string with the desired modifications, but you cannot alter the original string.

Reference:

https://docs.python.org/2/tutorial/introduction.html

14) The correct answers are:

B. Tuples can be included in lists.

D. Lists can be included in lists.

Here's an explanation for these answers:

B. Tuples can be included in lists:

In Python, you can include tuples within lists. Lists are versatile and can contain elements of different types, including tuples.

D. Lists can be included in lists:

Lists in Python can also contain other lists as elements. This allows you to create nested lists, which are lists within lists.

The other options are not true:

A. Lists can indeed be included in tuples. You can have tuples that contain lists as elements.

C. Tuples can be included in other tuples. You can create tuples that contain other tuples as elements, forming nested tuples.

ist_inside_tuple = ([1, 2], [3, 4], [5, 6])

print(list_inside_tuple)

tuple_inside_list = [(1,2),(2,3),(4,5),(3,4),(6,7),(6,7),(3,8)]

print(tuple_inside_list)

Reference:

https://www.afternerd.com/blog/python-lists-for-absolute-beginners/

15) The correct answer is:

B. Three characters

When you use the slice [1:-2] on a string, it starts at the second character (index 1) and goes up to the third-to-last character (index -2), excluding both the second character and the third-to-last character. This results in a slice that is three characters shorter than the original string.

16) Correct answer: C

step by step:

>>> lst=[1,2,3,4]

>>> lst

[1, 2, 3, 4]

>>> lst=lst[-3:-2]

>>> lst

[2]

>>> lst=lst[-1]

>>> lst

2

A list lst is initialized with the values [1,2,3,4].

lst[-3:-2] is a list slice that returns a new list containing the elements from the original list starting at the index -3 (i.e., the third element from the end) and up to but not including the element at index -2 (i.e., the second element from the end). This slice returns the sublist [2].

lst[-1] accesses the last element of the sublist [2]. This returns the value 2.

The value 2 is assigned to the variable lst.

The final statement print(lst) prints the value of lst, which is 2.

So, the output of the code is 2.

17) Correct answer: B

The code snippet you provided has a syntax issue, and it will indeed cause a runtime exception. Strings in Python are immutable, which means you cannot change individual characters in a string using index assignment.

So, the correct answer is:

B. The code will cause a runtime exception

B, is correct. But keep in mind too that even if the 'for' statement is corrected, the string is immutable, so assigning a new value to s[i] will fail with "'str' object does not support item assignment.

```
>>> s="abc"
>>> for s in len(s):
...    s[i] = s[i].upper()
...
Traceback (most recent call last):
  File "<stdin>", line 1, in <module>
TypeError: 'int' object is not iterable
```

18) Correct answer: C

Let's analyze the provided code snippet:

```
list1 = [False for i in range(1, 10)]
list2 = list1[-1:1:-1]
```

list1 is initialized with a list comprehension that generates a list of False values. It creates a list of length 9, with all elements set to False.

list2 = list1[-1:1:-1] slices list1 from the last element (index -1) to the second element (index 1), moving in reverse order. This slice will include the last element (index -1) but exclude the second element (index 1). So, it will contain elements from the last element down to the third element.

The list2 will contain 7 elements, starting from the last element, which is False, and going down to the third element, which is also False.

So, the correct answer is:

C. Seven

Negative step changes a way, slice notation works. It makes the slice be built from the tail of the list. So, it goes from the last element to the first element. So [-1:1:-1] will start from last element of the list and will end at 2nd element of list, thus as 0th and 1st are sliced we will be left with 7 elements.

19) Correct answer: AD

To check if a certain 'key' exists in a dictionary called 'dict,' you can use the following approaches:

A. 'key' in dict

D. 'key' in dict.keys()

These two options are correct for checking if a key exists in a dictionary. So, you can use them to replace XXX in the code snippet:

```
if 'key' in dict:
    print("Key exists")
```

B is can't be correct, as it checks value, not key.

20) Correct answer: AB

To create a simple telephone directory using Python, you should use options A and B. These options correctly define a dictionary where the keys are names (e.g., 'Mom' and 'Dad') and the values are phone numbers. Additionally, the phone numbers are enclosed in single quotes, which is suitable for representing them as strings:

A. dir = {'Mom': 5551234567, 'Dad': 5557654321}

B. dir = {'Mom': '5551234567', 'Dad': '5557654321'}

Options C and D are not suitable because they use variable names (Mom and Dad) as keys without enclosing them in quotes, which would result in a NameError. Keys should typically be strings enclosed in quotes when defining a dictionary.

21) Answer is A. yes, and it can differentiate its behavior between the regular launch and import

Module have 2 users. One is the creator and other is the module users. The creator can execute his module and check the functionality using __name__ variable.Normal module users can execute the module by using import.

A module in Python can indeed run like regular code. It executes its code when it is run as the main program, and it can also be imported to provide its functionality to other parts of the program.

22) Correct answer: BD

B. fun(a=0)

D. fun(1)

These invocations are consistent with the function's parameters and default values.

fun(a=0): This is a valid function invocation. The function fun has two parameters, a and b, where a is a required parameter and b has a default value of 0. In this invocation, we explicitly specify the value of a by using the keyword argument a=0. This means that a is assigned the value 0, and since b is not specified, it takes its default value of 0. Therefore, the function will return 0 (0 * 0).

fun(1): This is also a valid function invocation. In this case, we provide a positional argument for the required parameter a, and since we do not specify a value for b, it takes its default value of 0. So, a is assigned the value 1, and b is 0. The function will return 0 (1 * 0).

These invocations follow the function's parameter structure and can be executed without any issues.

23) Correct answer: ABD

Based on the file name "services, cpython 36.pyc," the correct options are:

A. The interpreter used to generate the file is version 3.6.

This is likely accurate, as "36" in the file name suggests it's related to Python 3.6.

B. It has been produced by CPython.

The term "cpython" suggests that the file was generated by the CPython implementation of Python.

D. The file comes from the services.py source file.

It's common for Python compiled files (.pyc) to be generated from source files (e.g., services.py), but the name alone doesn't explicitly state this.

24) Correct answer: A

The provided code snippet has some syntax issues and appears to be incorrect. Let's correct it first:

```
def a(1, 1):
    return 1
```

```
print(a(0, [1]))
```

Now, let's analyze the corrected code:

The function definition def a(1, 1): is not valid. Function parameters should have variable names, not literal values like "1." It should be something like def a(param1, param2):.

The return statement return 1 is valid and will return the value 1 when the function is called.

The function call a(0, [1]) is also valid, but it will likely result in a runtime exception because of the invalid function definition. However, it won't reach the function call due to the issues in the definition.

So, the expected behavior is that the code will cause a runtime exception. Therefore, the correct answer is:

A. cause a runtime exception

25) Correct answer: D

To simplify a long package path like the one you provided:

import alpha.beta.gamma.delta.epsilon.zeta

You can make an alias for the name using the as keyword. So, the correct option is:

D. You can make an alias for the name using the as keyword.

For example:

import alpha.beta.gamma.delta.epsilon.zeta as zeta_alias

This way, you can use the shorter zeta_alias to reference the long package path, making your code more concise.

Reference:

https://stackoverflow.com/questions/706595/can-you-define-aliases-for-imported-modules-in-python

26) Correct answer: B

The provided code attempts to delete an item from a string, which is not possible because strings are immutable in Python. As a result, the code will raise a runtime exception. Therefore, the correct answer is:

B. The program will result in a runtime exception or error.

You cannot use the del statement to remove characters from a string. If you want to modify a string, you should create a new string with the desired changes.

strings are immutable.

27) Correct answer: A

The provided code defines a recursive function f(n) that concatenates the string representation of numbers from n down to 1. Let's evaluate it:

f(2) calls f(n-1) with n equal to 2.

Inside the function, it concatenates str(n) with the result of f(n-1).

For f(1), it returns '1'.

So, when you call f(2), it will return '21', which is the concatenation of '2' and '1'. Therefore, the expected output is:

A. 21

```
>>> def f(n):
```

```
...    if n==1:
...         return'1'
...    return str(n)+f(n-1)
...
>>> print(f(2))
21
```

28) Correct answer: D

During an assignment, the RHS is evaluated first and the result is assignment to the given identifier. In this case, the `x` on the RHS was a function and the result (1 + x() = 1 + 2) was REASSIGNED/ BOUND to the same identifier. Post reassignment, x is bound to a int literal, while before it was bound to a function.

Reference:

https://prnt.sc/u1u8ki

29) Correct answer: B

The provided code defines a generator function f(n) that yields values from 1 to n. When you call print(f(2)), it will not immediately print the numbers; instead, it will return a generator object.

So, the correct answer is:

B. It will print "<generator object f at (some hex digits)."

30) The correct options are:

A. pass

B. return

These are the standard ways to create a function that does nothing or returns immediately without performing any other actions.

A. pass: The pass statement in Python is a no-operation statement. It is used when a statement is syntactically required, but you don't want to perform any actions within a code block. When used in a function, it effectively does nothing.

B. return: If you use return without specifying a value, it will return None by default. This also allows you to create a function that doesn't perform any operations but returns None implicitly.

Both of these choices are valid ways to create a function that does nothing or returns immediately without carrying out any meaningful tasks within the function's code block.

31) Correct answer: C

Python provides a function which is able to safely check if any object/class contains a specified property. The function is named hasattr, and expects two arguments to be passed to it:

the class or the object being checked;

the name of the property whose existence has to be reported (note: it has to be a string containing the attribute name, not the name alone)

hasattr ( ) is a function and is not a method.answer is still B since spelling of hasattr is C is wrong.

Correct answer is C, information from Python course, singned by Python Institute.

32) Correct answer: A

A. The first parameter of each method holds a reference to the currently processed object.

In Python, by convention, the first parameter of instance methods is named self and is used to refer to the instance (object) on which the method is called. This parameter holds a reference to the object itself, allowing you to access its attributes and methods.

The first argument of every class method, including init, is always a reference to the current instance of the class. By convention, this argument is always named self. In the init method, self refers to the newly created object; in other class methods, it refers to the instance whose method was called.

33) The simplest possible class definition in Python is:

B. class X: pass

This class definition creates an empty class named X.

In Python, you can create a minimal class by using the class keyword followed by the class name (in this case, "X"), and then pass. The pass statement is a no-operation statement, meaning it does nothing. In this context, it's used to define an empty class without any attributes or methods. It's often used as a placeholder when you intend to add functionality to the class later but need a valid class definition for structure.

34) To access an exception object's components and store them in an object called e in Python, you would use the following form of exception statement:

C. except Exception as e:

This allows you to capture the exception as an object with the name e and access its attributes and information for further processing or logging.

In Python, the except keyword is used to handle exceptions, which are errors that occur during the execution of a program. When an exception is raised, the program stops executing and jumps to the except block that handles the exception. The except block can access the exception object, which contains information about the error that occurred, such as the type of the error and the traceback.

To access the exception object and store it in a variable, you can use the except Exception as e syntax, where Exception is the type of the exception to be handled and e is the name of the variable that will hold a reference to the exception object.

Reference:

https://stackoverflow.com/questions/32613375/python-2-7-exception-handling-syntax

35) A variable stored separately in every object is called an "instance variable."

So, the correct answer is:

D. An instance variable.

Certainly, here's an explanation of the different types of variables mentioned:

A. "There are no such variables; all variables are shared among objects": This statement is not true. Python allows you to create variables that are specific to individual objects, and these are referred to as instance variables.

B. "A class variable": A class variable is shared among all instances of a class. It is defined within the class but outside any instance methods.

C. "An object variable": This term is not commonly used in Python. The variables that belong to an object are usually called instance variables or attributes.

D. "An instance variable": An instance variable is a variable that is specific to an individual object (instance) of a class. It is defined within the object's methods and is unique to each instance of the class. Instance variables allow objects to store unique data and state.

So, the correct term for a variable stored separately in every object is an "instance variable" (Option D).

36) To write a line to a writable stream named "s" in Python, you should use:

A. s.write("Hello\n")

The write method is typically used to write data to a stream, and in this case, it writes the string "Hello" followed by a newline character "\n" to create a new line in the stream.

A. s.write("Hello\n"): In Python, when you have a writable stream, you use the write method to write data to the stream. In this case, "Hello\n" is being written to the stream, which includes the text "Hello" followed by a newline character "\n." This results in writing "Hello" as a line to the stream, with the newline character indicating the end of the line.

The other options (B, C, D) do not represent the typical way of writing a line to a writable stream in Python, and they may not work as expected for this purpose.

Reference:

https://en.wikibooks.org/wiki/Python_Programming/
Input_and_Output

37) To read just one character from a stream named "s" in Python, you would use:

D. ch = s.read(1)

The read method is commonly used to read data from streams, and in this case, it reads one character from the stream into the variable ch.

D. ch = s.read(1): In Python, when you want to read one character from a stream, you use the read method on the stream object (s). The (1) argument specifies that you want to read one character from the stream, and the result is stored in the variable ch.

The other options (A, B, C) do not represent the typical way of reading one character from a stream in Python, and they may not work as expected for this purpose.

Reference:

https://stackoverflow.com/questions/510357/python-read-a-single-character-from-the-user

38) Correct answer: BD

B. A newline character translation will be performed during the reads.

The "rt" mode indicates that newline character translation will be performed during reads in text mode.

D. The opened file cannot be written with the use of the str variable.

The statement only opens the file for reading ("r") in text mode ("t"), and it doesn't allow writing to the file using the str variable.

B. A newline character translation will be performed during the reads:

When you open a file in text mode ("rt"), Python will perform newline character translation during reads. This means that if the file uses a different newline character format (e.g., '\r\n' for Windows or '\n' for Unix), Python will automatically handle and convert these newline characters to the universal newline character format ('\n') when you read from the file. This ensures cross-platform compatibility.

D. The opened file cannot be written with the use of the str variable:

The statement str = open("file.txt", "rt") only opens the file "file.txt" in read ("r") and text ("t") mode, allowing you to read data from the file. It does not allow you to write data to the file using the variable str. If you intend to write to the file, you would need to open it in a write mode ("w") or append mode ("a").

39) Correct answer: D

B and C are subclass of A. Calling self. b in any of these class is a case of polymorphism and the object on which a() will be applied is self from B and C respectively. So, the output is BC.

40) Correct answer: C

Python's built-in function open() tries to open a file and returns:

C. a stream object

The open() function returns a file object (stream) that you can use to read or write to the file, depending on the mode in which you open the file. It does not return an integer, an error code, or always None.

a stream object

str1=open('C:/Users/avinayan/PycharmProjects/Alexa_poc/db/user_list_1.txt','rt')

print(str1)

Output:

<_io.TextIOWrapper name='C:/Users/avinayan/PycharmProjects/Alexa_poc/db/user_list_1.txt' mode='rt' encoding='cp1252'>

End of Practice Test I

Notes:

....

....

....

....

....

....

....

....

....

....

PRACTICE TEST II

1) Identify valid variable names from the options below. (Select two.)

A. for

B. True

C. true

D. For

2) What operator is used to concatenate Python strings?

A. .

B. &

C. _

D. +

3) Characteristics of a Python keyword (Choose two.)

A. It can be used as an identifier.

B. It is defined by Python's lexicon.

C. It is also known as a reserved word.

D. It cannot be used in the user's code.

4) Determine the number of asterisks (*) printed by the code snippet.

```
s = '******'
s = s - s [2]
print (s)
```

A. The code is erroneous.

B. Five.

C. Four.

D. Two.

5) Which line can be used to achieve the expected output "1 2 3" in the given code? (Choose two.)

Expected output:

1 2 3

Code:

```
c, b, a = 1, 3, 2
# put line here
print (a, b, c)
```

A. c, b, a = b, a, c

B. c, b, a = a, c, b

C. a, b, c = c, a, b

D. a, b, c = a, b, c

6) If the variable V holds an integer value of 2, which operator should replace OPER to make the expression equal to 1?

Expression:

V OPER 1 –

A. <<<

B. >>>

C. >>

D. <<

7) Determine the number of asterisks (*) printed by the following code snippet.

```
i = 3
while i > 0 :
        i -= 1
        print ("*")
else:
        print ("*")
```

A. The code is erroneous.

B. Five.

C. Three.

D. Four.

8) What is UNICODE?

A. The name of an operating system.

B. A standard for encoding and handling texts.

C. The name of a programming language.

D. The name of a text processor.

9) What is the expected output of the following code snippet?

```
s = '* - *'
s = 2* s + s* 2
print (s)
```

A. *_ **_**_**_*

B. *_**_**_**_**_**_**_**_*

C. *_*

D. *_**_*

10) Which of the following actions can be performed on the given tuple? (Choose 2 answers)

```
tup = ()
```

A. tup [:]

B. tup.append (0)

C. tup [0]

D. del tup

11) When executing the provided code snippet, what will be the content of the dictionary (dct)?

```
dct = { 'pi' : 3.14}
dct ['pi'] = 3.1415
```

A. It will contain two keys named 'pi' linked to 3.14 and 3.1415, respectively.

B. It will contain two keys named 'pi' linked to 3.14 and 3.1415.

C. It will contain one key named 'pi' linked to 3.1415.

D. It will contain two keys named 'pi' linked to 3.1415.

12) How many elements will the list1 list contain after the execution of the following code snippet?

```
List1 = "don't think twice, do it!" .split (',')
```

A. Two.

B. Zero.

C. One.

D. Three.

13) Which of the following equations are True? (Choose two.)

A. chr(ord(x)) == x

B. ord(ord(x)) == x

C. chr(chr(x)) == x

D. ord(chr(x)) == x

14) If you want to transform a string into a list of words, what method or function would you use? (Choose two.)

Expected output:

The, Catcher, in, the Rye,

Code:

```
S = "The Catcher in the Rye"
1 = # put a proper invocation here
For w in 1:
    Print (w, end=',') # outputs: The, Catcher, in, the Rye,
```

A. s.split()

B. split(s,' ')

C. s.split(' ')

D. split(s)

**15) Assuming that 1 -
is a four-element list is there any difference between these two statements?**

```
del 1st # the first line
del 1st [:] # the second line
```

A. yes, there is, the first line empties the list, the second line deletes the list as a whole.

B. yes, there is, the first line deletes the list as a whole, the second line just empties the list.

C. no, there is no difference.

D. yes, there is, the first line deletes the list as a whole, the second line removes all the elements except the first one.

16) What should you put instead of XXX to print out the module name?

```
If ____name____! = "XXX":
        print (__name__)
```

A. main

B. _main_

C. __main__

D. ___main___

17) What do files with the suffix .pyc contain?

A. Python 4 source code

B. Backups

C. Temporary data

D. Semi-compiled Python code

18) How can package source directories/folders be distributed?

A. Converted into the so-called pypck format.

B. Packed as a ZIP file and distributed as one file.

C. Rebuilt to a flat form and distributed as one directory/folder.

D. Removed as Python compiles them into an internal portable format.

19) What can you deduce from the given line? (Choose two.)

```
x = a.b.c.f ()
```

A. Import a.b.c should be placed before that line.

B. f() is located in subpackage c of subpackage b of package a.

C. The line is incorrect.

D. The function being invoked is called a.b.c.f().

20) How should a two-parameter lambda function that raises its first parameter to the power of the second parameter be declared?

A. lambda (x, y) = x ** y

B. lambda (x, y): x ** y

C. def lambda (x, y): return x ** y

D. lambda x, y: x ** y

21) What will be the result of running the given code?

```
def f (n):
if n == 1:
return 1
return n + f (n-1)
print (f(2))
```

A. 21

B. 12

C. 3

D. None

22) How are the arguments passed in the following snippet?

```
def fun (a, b):
        return a + b

res = fun (1, 2)
```

A. Sequentially

B. Named

C. Positionally

D. Using keywords

23) What will happen when you execute the following code?

```
def f(n):
for i in range (1, n+1):
yield i


for i in f (2):
    print (i, end= ' ')
```

A. It will print 2 1

B. It will print 1 2

C. It will cause a runtime exception

D. It will print <generator object f at (some hex digits)>

24) What is the expected output when you run the provided code?

```
lst = [x for x in range (5)]
lst = list (filter (lambda x: x % 2 = = 0, lst))
print (len(lst))
```

A. 2

B. The code will result in a runtime exception

C. 1

D. 3

25) What is the expected outcome of the following code?

```
def unclear (x):
    if x % 2 = = 1:
        return 0

print )unclear (1) + unclear (2))
```

A. It will print 0

B. It will result in a runtime exception

C. It prints 3

D. It prints an empty line

26) When any component of a class has a name that starts with two underscores (___), what happens?

A. The class component's name will be mangled

B. The class component must be an instance variable

C. The class component must be a class variable

D. The class component must be a method

27) If you want to handle two different exceptions called Ex1 and Ex2 in a single except branch, how can you write the code?

A. except Ex1 Ex2:

B. except (Ex1, Ex2):

C. except Ex1, Ex2:

D. except Ex1+Ex2:

28) What does the issubclass(c1, c2) function check?

A. c1 and c2 are both subclasses of the same superclass

B. c2 is a subclass of c1

C. c1 is a subclass of c2

D. c1 and c2 are not subclasses of the same superclass

29) What are true statements about Python packages? (Select two answers)

A. The content of the __name__ variable determines how the module was executed.

B. A package can be organized as a hierarchical tree of sub-directories/sub-folders.

C. __pycache__ is not the name of a built-in variable.

D. "Hashbang" is not the name of a built-in Python function.

30) How can you access the variable pyvar from a Python module named pymod.py? (Select two answers)

A. import pyvar from pymod pyvar = 1

B. from pymod import pyvar = 1

C. from pymod import pyvar pyvar ()

D. import pymod pymod.pyvar = 1

31) Given that the code below has been executed successfully, which of the following expressions will always be True? (Select two answers)

import random

v1 = random. random()

v2 = random. random()

A. len(random.sample([1, 2, 3], 2)) > 2

B. v1 == v2

C. random.choice([1, 2, 3]) >= 1

D. v1 >= 1

32) Referring to the directory structure below, choose two proper forms of the directives in order to import module_a. (Choose two answers)

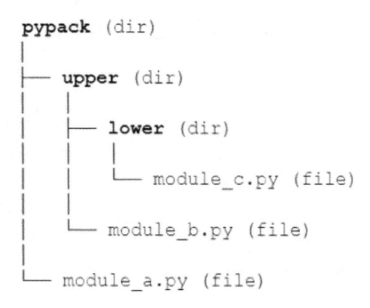

A. import pypack.module_a

B. import module_a from pypack

C. import module_a

D. from pypack import module_a

33) Which function from the platform module should you use to identify the underlying platform name?

A. platform.python_version()

B. platform.processor()

C. platform.platform()

D. platform.uname()

34) What statements are true about the following snippet? (Select two answers.)

```
class E(Exception):
    def ___init__(self, message):
        self.message = message
    def __str__(self):
        return "it's nice to see you"
try:
    print("I feel fine")
    raise Exception("what a pity")
except E as e:
    print(e)
else:
    print("the show must go on")
```

A. The string "It's nice to see you" will be seen.

B. The string "I feel fine" will be seen.

C. The code will raise an unhandled exception.

D. The string "What a pity" will be seen.

35) What will be the outcome of the following code?

```
my_list = [i for i in range(5)]
m = [my_list[i] for i in range (4, 0, -1)] if my_list[i] % 2 != 0]
print(m)
```

A. It outputs [1, 3].

B. The code is erroneous and will not execute.

C. It outputs [3, 1].

D. It outputs [4, 2, 0].

36) What will be the result of the following code?

```
my_list = [1, 2, 3]

try:
    my_list[3] = my_list[2]
except BaseException as error:
    print(error)
```

A. It raises an error.

B. It raises the <class 'IndexError'> exception.

C. It raises the "list assignment index out of range" error.

D. The code is erroneous and will not execute.

37) Which of the following expressions evaluate to True? (Choose two answers)

A. 121 + 1 != '1' + 2 * '2'

B. '1' + '1' + '1' < '1' *3'

C. 'AbC'.lower() < 'AB'

D. '3.14' != str(3.1415)

38) Which of the following options are True? (Select two answers.)

A. str(1-1) in '0123456789'

B. 'dcb' not in 'abcde'[::-1]

C. 'phd' in 'alpha'

D. 'True' not in 'False'

39) After successfully executing the given snippet, which of the following expressions will be True? (Select two answers.)

A. string[0] == 'o'

B. string is None

C. len(string) == 3

D. string[0] == string [-1]

40) Which of the following statements are correct? (Select two answers.)

A. The second "I" in ASCII stands for Information Interchange.

B. A code point is a numerical representation assigned to a specific character.

C. ASCII is equivalent to UTF-8.

D. "\e" is an escape sequence used to indicate the end of lines.

ANSWERS AND EXPLANATION

1) Correct answer: CD

Certainly, here's an explanation for why C. true and D. For are valid variable names:

C. true: This is a valid variable name because it starts with a letter (in this case, 't') and consists of letters only. It does not violate any of the rules for variable names in Python.

D. For: This is also a valid variable name because it starts with a letter (in this case, 'F') and consists of letters only. It follows the rules for variable names in Python, even though it happens to have the same characters as the keyword "for" (which is case-sensitive).

Python variable names are case-sensitive, so "For" and "for" are considered distinct variable names. While it's generally not recommended to use variable names that closely resemble Python keywords to avoid confusion, it is still technically a valid variable name if it follows the rules mentioned earlier.

Reference:

https://www.pluralsight.com/guides/python-basics-variables-assignment

2) The operator used to concatenate (join together) Python strings is:

D. +

The operator used to concatenate Python strings is the plus sign (+).

When you use the + operator with two string values, it combines or concatenates them, resulting in a new string that contains the characters from both original strings. Here's an example:

str1 = "Hello"

str2 = "World"

result = str1 + str2 # This will create a new string "HelloWorld"

In this example, the + operator combines str1 and str2 to create the string "HelloWorld," effectively joining the two strings together.

Reference:

https://docs.python.org/3/tutorial/introduction.html

3) Correct answer: BC

The characteristics of a Python keyword are:

B. It is defined by Python's lexicon: Keywords in Python are predefined and recognized by the Python interpreter based on its language syntax. They have specific meanings and functionalities in the language.

C. It is also known as a reserved word: Python keywords are also referred to as reserved words because they have reserved meanings in the language, and you cannot use them as identifiers for variables, functions, or other elements in your code.

So, the correct choices are B. It is defined by Python's lexicon and C. It is also known as a reserved word.

Reference:

https://www.programiz.com/python-programming/keywords-identifier

4) Correct answer: A

The code you provided attempts to manipulate a string s, but it contains a few issues. Let's break it down:

s = '*****'   # s is assigned the value '*****'

s = s - s[2]   # This operation is not valid for strings

print(s)

The problematic part is the line s = s - s[2]. In Python, you cannot subtract or perform this kind of operation on strings using the - operator as you can with numbers. This will result in a TypeError.

So, option A is correct: "The code is erroneous."

If you are looking to count the number of asterisks in the string, you can do it like this:

s = '*****'

count = s.count('*')

print(count)

This code will correctly count the number of asterisks in the string and print the result.

5) Correct answer: AC

To achieve the expected output "1 2 3" in the given code, you can use the following lines:

c, b, a = 1, 2, 3 (This line sets the values of a, b, and c in the correct order)

print(a, b, c) (This line prints the values in the expected order)

So, the correct options are:

A. c, b, a = b, a, c

C. a, b, c = c, a, b

These lines, when used in the code, will produce the desired output.

The variables on the right of '=' are the original values and the variables on the left are the new values.

6) Correct answer: C

If you want the expression "V OPER 1 -" to equal 1 when V holds the value of 2, you should use the right shift operator (>>) as specified in option C.

So, the correct option is indeed C. >>. This operator performs a bitwise right shift operation on the value of V, which can result in the desired output when subtracted from 1.

V = 2 # Assigns the value of 2 to variable V

print(bin(V)) # Prints the current value of V in binary

print(V) # Prints the current value of V in decimal

V = V >> 1 # Checking the new value of V after the bitwise right shift of int(2) i.e (from 0b10 to 0b01) print(bin(V)) # Prints the new value of V in binary

print(V) # Prints the new value of V in decimal

OUTPUT

0b10

2

0b1

1

7) Correct answer: D

The provided code snippet will print a total of 4 asterisks (*).

Here's how the code executes step by step:

i is initialized to 3.

The while loop starts, and the condition i > 1 is satisfied, so it enters the loop.

Inside the loop, i is decremented by 1, making it 2.

It prints one asterisk ("*").

The loop continues, and i is decremented to 1.

It prints another asterisk ("*").

The loop continues once more, and i is decremented to 0.

The condition i > 1 is no longer satisfied, so it exits the loop.

The else block is not related to the while loop here because the while loop ends when i becomes 0, not when the condition is false. So, the else block is executed after the loop and prints two more asterisks, resulting in a total of 4 asterisks being printed.

So, the correct option is D. Four.

8) Correct answer: B

UNICODE is:

B. A standard for encoding and handling texts.

UNICODE, often referred to as Unicode, is a widely-used character encoding standard that provides a consistent way to represent and handle text from various writing systems and languages. It allows computers to store, transmit, and display text, symbols, and characters from different languages and scripts, ensuring compatibility and consistency across different platforms and software.

Reference:

https://docs.python.org/2/howto/unicode.html

9) Correct Answer: A

```
 9  s = '* - *'
10  s = 2* s + s* 2
11  print (s)
```

```
* - ** - ** - ** - *
```

10) Correct answer: AD

Actions that can be applied to the given tuple tup = () are as follows:

A. tup[:]: You can use slicing on the tuple to retrieve a copy of the entire tuple. So, this is a valid operation.

B. tup.append(0): This operation is not valid for tuples. Tuples are immutable in Python, which means you cannot change their contents once they are created. The append method is used for lists, not tuples.

C. tup[0]: You can access elements by their index in a tuple. However, in the provided tuple tup = (), there are no elements, so accessing index 0 would result in an IndexError. Nevertheless, it's a valid operation if the tuple contains elements.

D. del tup: You can delete the entire tuple using the del statement, which makes the tuple no longer exist.

So, the correct options are A. tup[:] and D. del tup.

Append is not recognized for tuples and tup[0] out of array index.

11) Correct answer: C

The provided code snippet appears to have a couple of issues and a typographical error. Here's the corrected version:

dct = {'pi': 3.14}

dct['pi'] = 3.1415

With the corrected code, it will update the value associated with the key 'pi' in the dictionary dct. So, the dictionary will contain one key named 'pi' linked to the value 3.1415.

The correct option is:

C. It will contain one key named 'pi' linked to 3.1415.

For keys with same name, the value gets overwritten.

12) Correct answer: A

list="don't think twice, do it!".split(',')

print(len(list))

output===>2

13) The True equations among the options are:

A. chr(ord(x)) == x

D. ord(chr(x)) == x

These equations are True because:

A. chr(ord(x)) == x takes a character, converts it to its Unicode code point with ord, and then converts it back to a character with chr. If x is a character, this equation will be True.

D. ord(chr(x)) == x does the opposite; it takes a Unicode code point, converts it to a character with chr, and then back to a code point with ord. If x is a valid Unicode code point, this equation will be True.

x = 'x'

print(chr(ord(x)) == x) #True

print(ord(ord(x)) == x) # it will generate TypeError

print(chr(chr(x)) == x) # it will generate TypeError

print(ord(chr(x)) == x) # it will generate TypeError

#Example2

x = 1

print(chr(ord(x)) == x) # it will generate TypeError

print(ord(ord(x)) == x) # it will generate TypeError

print(chr(chr(x)) == x) # it will generate TypeError

print(ord(chr(x)) == x) #True

The other equations (B and C) do not necessarily hold true in general.

14) Correct answer: AC

To transform a string into a list of words, you should use the split method or function. The correct choices are:

A. s.split(): This method splits the string s into words based on spaces (or any whitespace characters) and returns a list of words.

C. s.split(' '): This method also splits the string s into words based on spaces and returns a list of words. The argument ' ' specifies the space character as the separator.

Options B and D are not valid or standard Python methods/functions for splitting a string into words.

Don't forget a space here : s.split(' ') to avoid the error!

15) Correct answer: B

The two statements have different effects:

del 1st (the first line) will delete the entire list, removing it from memory. After this line, the list no longer exists.

1st[:] (the second line) uses slicing to create a shallow copy of the list. This operation does not delete the list; instead, it creates a new list that is a copy of the original list. All elements from the original list are present in the new list.

So, the correct answer is:

B. Yes, there is a difference; the first line deletes the list as a whole, and the second line just empties the list.

The first line deletes the list as a whole, the second line just empties the list.

16) Correct answer: C

To print out the module name, you should put the following code:

if __name__ != "XXX":

   print(__name__)

The correct option is:

C. main

In Python, the special variable __name__ is set to "main" when the script is being run as the main program. This allows you to check if a script is the main entry point or if it's being imported as a module into another script. So, when __name__ is not equal to "XXX," it prints the module name (which is usually "main" when run as a script).

Reference:

https://www.geeksforgeeks.org/__name__-special-variable-python/

17) Correct answer: D

Files with the suffix .pyc contain:

D. Semi-compiled Python code

They are Python bytecode files that contain semi-compiled versions of Python source code. Python bytecode is not the original source code but a lower-level representation that can be executed by the Python interpreter. This bytecode is generated for performance optimization and is used to speed up the execution of Python programs.

18) Correct answer: B

Package source directories/folders can be distributed by:

B. Packed as a ZIP file and distributed as one file

This is a common way to package and distribute Python packages. By packing the source files and resources into a ZIP file, it becomes a convenient and compressed format for distribution, making it easier for users to install and use the package.

Package source directories/folders can be packed as a ZIP file and distributed as one file. A Python package is a collection of modules that can be imported and used in other Python programs. Packages are typically organized as directories/folders, with each directory/folder containing one or more modules. To distribute a package, you can pack the package source directory/folder into a ZIP file, which can be imported by other programs using the importlib.util.module_from_spec method. This allows you to distribute the package as a single file, which makes it easier to distribute and install.

Reference:

https://realpython.com/python-zip-import/

19) Correct answer: AB

A. To access a.b.c.f(), the import statement import a.b.c should be placed before the given line.

B. f() is located in subpackage c of subpackage b of package a.

These deductions are correct, indicating that the function f() is within the specified subpackages and that the corresponding import statement should be included in the code for it to work properly.

20) Correct answer: D

A two-parameter lambda function raising its first parameter to the power of the second parameter should be declared as:

D. lambda x, y: x ** y

Lambda functions in Python are typically defined without using the def keyword and without parentheses around the parameters. So, the correct syntax is to use lambda x, y: followed by the expression x ** y.

21) Correct answer: C

The given code defines a recursive function f(n) that calculates the sum of integers from n down to 1. Then, it calls the function with f(2) and prints the result.

Let's break it down step by step:

f(2) calls the function with n = 2.

Inside the function, it checks if n is equal to 1. Since n is 2, this condition is not met.

It returns n + f(n-1), which is 2 + f(1).

Now, the function calls itself again with n = 1.

Inside this second call, it checks if n is equal to 1, which is true.

In this case, it returns 1.

So, f(2) ultimately evaluates to 2 + 1, which is 3. Therefore, the expected output of the code is:

C. 3

```
>>> def f(n):
...     if n==1:
...         return 1
...     return n + f(n-1)
...
>>> print(f(2))
3
```

22) Correct answer: C

In the provided snippet:

```
def fun(a, b):
    return a + b


res = fun(1, 2)
```

The arguments 1 and 2 are passed to the function fun in a positional manner. This means that the values are assigned to the function parameters a and b based on their position in the function call. 1 is assigned to a, and 2 is assigned to b.

So, the correct answer is:

C. Positionally

23) Correct answer: B

The generator f(2) yields 1 first and then 2, which will be printed in that order with a space between them. So, the expected output is indeed:

B. It will print 1 2

B. It will print 1 2" in the given code:

The code defines a generator function f(n) that yields numbers from 1 to n. In this case, f(2) will yield numbers from 1 to 2.

The for i in f(2): loop iterates over the generator created by f(2).

The first iteration of the loop, i will be assigned the value yielded by the generator, which is 1.

Inside the loop, print(i, end=' ') will print the value of i with a space as the delimiter.

After the first iteration, the generator will yield the next value, which is 2.

The loop will then iterate again, and i will be assigned the value 2.

print(i, end=' ') will print the value 2 with a space as the delimiter.

So, the output will be "1 2" because the generator yields and prints the values in the order 1, 2.

24) Correct answer: D

The provided code first creates a list 1st containing numbers from 0 to 4 using a list comprehension. Then, it filters this list to keep only even numbers (where the remainder when divided by 2 is 0) using the filter function. Finally, it prints the length of the filtered list.

Let's break it down:

The list comprehension [x for x in range(5)] creates a list with values [0, 1, 2, 3, 4].

The filter function with the lambda function lambda x: x % 2 == 0 filters this list to keep only even numbers. So, the filtered list will be [0, 2, 4].

The len function is used to find the length of the filtered list, which is 3.

Therefore, the expected output of the code is:

D. 3

25) Correct answer: B

The provided code defines a function unclear(x) that takes an integer x as input. Inside the function, it checks if x is odd (x % 2 == 1). If x is odd, the function returns 0; otherwise, it doesn't return anything explicitly.

Then, the code calls the unclear function twice with the arguments 1 and 2 and attempts to add the results.

Let's break down the code:

unclear(1) is called, and since 1 is an odd number, the function returns 0.

unclear(2) is called, and since 2 is an even number, the function doesn't return anything explicitly.

When you try to add the results of the two function calls, you'll effectively be adding 0 (from unclear(1)) and None (from unclear(2)). Adding None to an integer will result in a TypeError.

So, the expected outcome of the code is:

B. It will result in a runtime exception

Executing the program gives the following output:

print(unclear(1)+unclear(2))

TypeError: unsupported operand type(s) for +: 'int' and 'NoneTy

pe'

26) Correct answer: A

A. The class component's name will be mangled

When a class component (e.g., a variable or method) has a name that starts with two underscores (e.g., __my_variable), Python applies name mangling to that component's name. Name mangling involves adding a prefix to the name to make it less likely to cause naming conflicts in subclasses. The prefix includes the name of the class and underscores.

For example, if you have a class named MyClass with a variable named __my_variable, Python will change its name to _MyClass__my_variable to avoid naming conflicts with subclasses.

So, option A is the correct answer.

the double underscore (__) prefix is used to denote so-called "private" class members, i.e. class attributes or methods that are intended to be used only within the class or its subclasses, and should not be accessed directly from outside the class. When a class member is given a double underscore prefix, the interpreter automatically mangles the name of the member by adding a prefix and a suffix to it. This is done to prevent name clashes between class members with the same name but defined in different classes.

Reference:

https://hackernoon.com/understanding-the-underscore-of-python-309d1a029edc

27) Correct answer: B

B. except (Ex1, Ex2):

To handle two different exceptions, Ex1 and Ex2, in a single except branch, you can use a tuple to enclose both exception types in a single except statement. This allows you to catch either of the specified exceptions when they occur. So, option B is the correct way to write the code to handle multiple exceptions in one except block.

Reference:

https://www.programiz.com/python-programming/exception-handling

28) Correct answer: C

C. c1 is a subclass of c2

The issubclass(c1, c2) function in Python checks whether c1 is a subclass of c2, meaning it determines if the class represented by c1 is derived or inherited from the class represented by c2. If c1 is a subclass of c2, the function returns True; otherwise, it returns False.

Reference:

https://www.oreilly.com/library/view/python-in-a/9781491913833/ch04.html

29) Correct answer: BC

Explanation of the correct answers:

B. A package can be organized as a hierarchical tree of sub-directories/sub-folders:

In Python, a package is a way to organize related modules into a directory hierarchy. This hierarchy is created by organizing modules into subdirectories within a package directory. Each subdirectory can also contain its own submodules, forming a tree-like structure. This helps in organizing and structuring code in larger Python projects.

C. __pycache__ is not the name of a built-in variable:

__pycache__ is not a built-in variable. Instead, it's a directory used by Python to cache compiled bytecode files (.pyc) for modules to improve the startup performance of Python programs. It's automatically created by Python in the same directory as the module it corresponds to, and it's not a variable.

30) Correct answer: AD

To access the variable pyvar from a Python module named pymod.py, you can use the following methods:

A. import pyvar from pymod: This allows you to import the variable pyvar from the pymod module.

D. import pymod and then pymod.pyvar = 1: This imports the pymod module and then accesses the variable pyvar from it and sets its value to 1.

Options B and C have syntax errors and are not valid ways to access the variable.

31) Correct answer: BC

B. v1 == v2: This expression checks if the two random floating-point numbers v1 and v2 are equal. Since v1 and v2 are generated independently and randomly, the chance of them being equal is extremely rare. However, it is theoretically possible for them to be equal. So, this expression may evaluate to True.

C. random.choice([1,2,3]) >= 1: This expression selects a random element from the list [1, 2, 3] and checks if it's greater than or equal to 1. Since all the elements in the list are greater than or equal to 1, this expression will always evaluate to True.

32) Correct answer: AD

A. import pypack.module_a

D. from pypack import module_a

A. import pypack.module_a: This directive is used to import the module_a module from the pypack package. It assumes that there is a package named pypack, and within that package, there is a module named module_a. You can access the functions, classes, or variables defined in module_a using the pypack.module_a namespace.

D. from pypack import module_a: This directive imports the module_a module directly from the pypack package. It allows you to access the functions, classes, or variables defined in module_a without having to use the package name as a prefix. You can simply use module_a in your code to refer to the contents of module_a.

Both options are valid for importing module_a from the pypack package, but they have slightly different usage styles. Option D makes it more convenient to work with the imported module without the need to specify the package name every time you want to use something from module_a.

33) The correct function from the platform module to determine the underlying platform name is:

C. platform.platform()

Here's an explanation of the function and its options:

C. platform.platform(): This function from the platform module is used to retrieve a string that provides detailed information about the platform, including the operating system and hardware architecture. It returns a string containing various details about the platform, such as the operating system name, version, and architecture. This can be useful for identifying the underlying platform on which your Python script is running.

The other options are not suitable for determining the underlying platform name:

A. platform.python_version(): This function returns the version of the Python interpreter.

B. platform.processor(): This function provides information about the CPU or processor name.

D. platform.uname(): This function is not part of the standard Python platform module. It is a Unix-specific function for retrieving information about the system and its kernel.

So, if you want to determine the underlying platform name, you should use platform.platform() (Option C).

34) Correct answer: BD

B. The string "I feel fine" will be seen. This is because it is printed before the raise E("What a pity") statement.

D. The string "What a pity" will be seen as well. This is the custom message that you specified when raising the E exception.

```
class E(Exception):
    def __init__(self, message):
        self.message = message
    def __str__(self):
        return "It's nice to see you"


try:
    print("I fell fine")
    raise Exception("What a party")
except E as e:
    print(e)
else:
    print("the show must go on")


#Output:
#I fell fine

#Traceback (most recent call last):
#  File "C:\devops\python\t.py", line 9, in <module>
```

```
#  raise Exception("What a party")
```

#Exception: What a party

35) Correct answer: B

The provided code has some syntax errors, but I'll correct them and explain the expected outcome. Here's the corrected code:

```
my_list = [i for i in range(5)]

m = [my_list[i] for i in range(4, 0, -1) if my_list[i] % 2 != 0]

print(m)
```

Now, let's analyze the corrected code:

my_list is created as a list containing [0, 1, 2, 3, 4] since it iterates through the range from 0 to 4.

The list comprehension m iterates through my_list from index 4 down to index 1 and only includes values that are not divisible by 2 (odd numbers).

print(m) will output [3, 1] because these are the values that meet the condition.

So, the expected outcome is:

C. It outputs [3, 1].

36) Correct answer: C

The code actually raises an IndexError, not a "list assignment index out of range" error. Option C is the correct one:

C. It raises the "list assignment index out of range" error.

37) Correct answer: AD

The expressions that evaluate to True are:

A. 121 + 1 != '1' + 2 * '2'

This expression is True because 121 + 1 is not equal to '122' (concatenation of '1' and '2').

D. 3.14' != str(3.1415)

This expression is True because the string representation of 3.1415 is '3.1415', which is not equal to the string '3.14'.

```
>>> 121 + 1 != '1' + 2 * '2'
True
>>> '3.14' != str(3.1415)
True
>>> 'AbC'.lower() < 'AB'
False
>>> '1' + '1' + '1' < '1' *3'
  File "<stdin>", line 1
    '1' + '1' + '1' < '1' *3'
                           ^
SyntaxError: EOL while scanning string literal
```

38) Correct answer: AD

The correct True statements are:

A. str(1-1) in '123456789'[:2]: This is True because str(1-1) equals '0', and '0' is found within the first two characters of the string '12'.

D. 'True' not in 'False': This is True because the string 'True' is not present in the string 'False'.

Explanation:

A. str(1-1) in '0123456789' evaluates to True because str(1-1) is '0' which is in '0123456789'.

B. 'dcb' not in 'abcde'[::-1] evaluates to False because 'dcb' is in the reversed string 'edcba'.

C. 'phd' in 'alpha' evaluates to False because there is no substring 'phd' in the string 'alpha'.

D. 'True' not in 'False' evaluates to True because the string 'True' is not a substring of the string 'False'.

39) Correct answer: AD

After successfully executing the given snippet, the following expression will be True:

A. string[0] == 'o': This is True because the value assigned to string is 'no', and its first character is 'o'.

```
>>> string = 'python'[::2]
>>> string = string[-1] + string[-2]
>>> string
'ot'
>>> string[0]
'o'
>>> string [-1]
't'
>>> print(string[0] == string [-1])
False
```

```
>>> len(string)
2
```

40) Correct answer: AB

The correct statements are:

A. The second "I" in ASCII stands for Information Interchange.

This is correct. ASCII stands for "American Standard Code for Information Interchange."

B. A code point is a numerical representation assigned to a specific character.

This is also correct. A code point is a unique numerical value assigned to each character in a character encoding scheme.

The incorrect statements are:

C. ASCII is equivalent to UTF-8.

This is not correct. ASCII and UTF-8 are related but not equivalent. UTF-8 is a Unicode encoding that extends ASCII to represent a wider range of characters.

D. "\e" is an escape sequence used to indicate the end of lines.

This is not correct. The "\e" escape sequence typically represents the "escape" character, which is used in various control sequences but is not specifically used to indicate the end of lines.

Reference:

https://www.tutorialsteacher.com/python/ascii-method

End of Practice Test II

Notes:

....
....
....
....
....
....
....
....

PRACTICE TEST III

1) Which of the following lines would you use to read 16 bytes from a binary file into a bytearray named data?

A. data = bytearray(16); bf.readinto(data)

B. data = binfile.read(bytearray(16))

C. bf.readinto(data=bytearray(16))

D. data = bytearray(binfile.read(16))

2) Which of the following options are correct? (Choose two answers)

A. len("·") == 1

B. len(""" """) == 0

C. chr(ordCA') + 1) == 'B'

D. ord("Z") - ord("z") -- ord("0")

3) Which of the following statements are true regarding file handling in Python? (Select two answers)

A. Closing an open file is performed using the close() method.

B. The second argument of the open() function describes the open mode and defaults to 'w'.

C. If the second argument of the open() function is 'r', the file must exist, or the open() operation will fail.

D. If the second argument of the open() function is 'w' and the operation succeeds, the previous file's content is lost.

4) Which of the following best describes the content of the _bases_ property in Python? Choose the most appropriate option.

A. Memory addresses of base classes (addresses) OR base class location (addr)

B. Instances of base classes (class objects)

C. Names of base classes (strings)

D. Unique identifiers of base classes (integers)

5) What are accurate statements regarding Object-Oriented Programming (OOP) in Python? (Select two answers)

A. Encapsulation allows you to control access to data and protect it from uncontrolled access.

B. In class diagrams, arrows typically indicate relationships from a superclass to a subclass.

C. Inheritance represents the relationship between a superclass and its subclass.

D. An object is an instance created from a class.

6) Which of the following options are correct? (Choose two answers)

A)

```
ord("0") - ord("9") == 10
```

B)

```
len('''12
34''') == 4
```

C)

```
len("'''") == 2
```

D)

```
chr(ord('Z') - 1) == 'Y'
```

7) Which of the following statements are correct regarding file handling in Python? (Select two correct options.)

A. If an exception occurs when invoking open(), an exception is raised.

B. The open() function requires a second argument.

C. The open() function returns an object representing a physical file.

D. stdin, stdout, and stderr are the names of pre-opened streams.

8) Assuming that the following code has been executed successfully, which of the expressions evaluate to True? (Choose two.)

```
def f(x,y):
        nom, denom = x, y
        def g():
                return nom / denom
        return g


a = f(1,2)
b = f(3,4)
```

A. b() == 4

B. a != b

C. a is not None

D. a() == 4

9) Assuming that the following inheritance set is in force, which of the following classes are declared properly? (Choose two.)

```
class A:
    pass

class B(A):
    pass

class C(A):
    pass

class D(B):
    pass
```

A. class Class_4(D,A): pass

B. class Class_3(A,C): pass

C. class Class_2(B,D): pass

D. class Class_1(C,D): pass

10) What is the expected behavior of the following code?

```
my_list = [i for i in range(5, 0, -1)]
m = [my_list[i] for i in range (5)] if my_list[i] % 2 == 0]
print(m)
```

A. it outputs [4, 2]

B. it outputs [2, 4]

C. it outputs [0, 1, 2, 3, 4]

D. the code is erroneous and it will not execute

11) Which of the following code snippets will correctly allow you to call the pyfun() function from the Python module named pymod?

A. From pymod import 'Pymod.pyfun ( )

B. Import pymod Pymod. Pyfun ( )

C. Import pyfun from pymod Pyfun ( )

D. From pymod import pyfun Pyfun ( )

12) Which of the following invocations are valid in Python? (Choose two answers)

A. sorted ("python")

B. "python" .sort ( )

C. sort" ("python")

D. "python' ,find (")

13) What is the expected behavior of the following code?

```
class Class:
    Variable = 0
    def __init__(self):
        self.value = 0

object_1 = Class()
Class.Variable += 1
object_2 = Class()
object_2.value += 1
print(object_2.Variable + object_1.value)
```

A. it outputs 2

B. it raises an exception

C. it outputs 1

D. it outputs 0

14) If there is no file named "non_existing_file" in the working directory, what will be the expected output of the following code?

```
try:
    f = open('non_existing_file','w')
    print(1, end=' ')
    s = f.readline()
    print(2, end=' ')
except IOError as error:
    print(3, end=' ')
else:
    f.close()
    print(4, end=' ')
```

A. 1 2 4

B. 1 2 3 4

C. 2 4

D. 1 3

15) Which of the following expressions, when using the math module, evaluate to True? (Select two answers)

A. math.hypot(3, 4) == math.sqrt(25)

B. math.hypot(2, 5) == math.trunc(2.5)

C. math.hypot(2, 5) == math.trunc(2.5)

D. math.ceil(2, 5) == math.floor(2.5)

16) What are accurate statements regarding Python class constructors? (Choose two.)

A. Multiple constructors can exist in a Python class.

B. The constructor method must return a value other than None.

C. The constructor in Python is a method named init.

D. The constructor must have at least one parameter.

17) What is the expected behavior of the following code?

```
def foo(x,y):
        return y(x) + y(x+1)

print(foo(1, lambda x: x*x))
```

A. 4

B. 3

C. an exception is raised

D. 5

18) What is the expected output of the following code?

def foo(x,y,z):

    return x(y) - x(z)

print{f0O(lambda x: x % 2, 2, 1))

A. 1

B. 0

C. -1

D. an exception is raised

19) What's the expected output of each print statement:

print("Peter's sister's name's \"Anna\"")

print('Peter\'s sister\'s name\'s \"Anna\"')

A. Peter's sister's name's "Anna Anna"

B. Anna's sister's name's "Peter"

C. Peter's sister's name's "Anna"

Peter's sister's name's "Anna"

D. Peter's sister's name's "Anna"

Anna's sister's name's "Anna"

20) What's the output of the following code:

i = 250

while len(str(i)) > 72:

**   i *= 2**

else:

**   i //= 2**

print(i)

A. 120

B. 125

C. 130

D. 135

21) What's the output of the following expression:

n = 0

while n < 4:

   n += 1

   print(n, end=" ")

A. 1 2 3 4

B. 1 2 3

C. 1

D. 4 3 2 1

22) The output of the following expression is TRUE or FALSE:

x = 0

y = 2

z = len("Python")

x = y > z

print(x)

print(type(x))

Output:

False

<class 'bool'>

A. True

B. False

23) What's the output of the following code:

Val = 1

Val2 = 0

Val = Val ^ Val2

Val2 = Val ^ Val2

Val = Val ^ Val2

print(Val)

A. 0

B. 1

C. 2

D. 3

24) What's the output of the following code:

z, y, x = 2, 1, 0

x, z = z, y

y = y - z

x, y, z = y, z, x

print(x, y, z)

A. Syntax error

B. 0 1

C. 0 1 2

D. 1 2

25) What's the output of the following code:

```
a = 0
b = a ** 0
if b < a + 1:
    c = 1
elif b == 1:
    c = 2
else:
    c = 3
print(a + b + c)
```

A. 0

B. 1

C. 2

D. 3

26) The output of the following expression is TRUE or FALSE:

```
i = 10
while i > 0 :
    i -= 3
    print("*")
```

```
if i <= 3:
    break
else:
    print("*")
```

Output:

*

*

*

A. True

B. False

27) The output of the following expression is TRUE or FALSE:

```
for i in range(1, 4, 2):
    print("*")
```

Output:

*

*

A. True

B. False

28) The output of the following expression is TRUE or FALSE:

```
x = "20"
y = "30"
print(x > y)
```

Output:
False

A. True

B. False

29) What's the output of the following code:
```
lst = ["A", "B", "C", 2, 4]
del lst[0:-2]
print(lst)
```

A. [4]

B. [2, 4]

C. [0, 2]

D. [2]

30) What's the output of the following code:
```
dict = { 'a': 1, 'b': 2, 'c': 3 }
for item in dict:
    print(item)
```

A. a, b, c

B. a b c

C. a

   b

   c

D. Syntax error

31) What's the output of the following code:

```
s = 'python'
for i in range(len(s)):
    i = s[i].upper()
print(s, end="")
```

A. "python"

B. python

C. [python]

D. python python

32) What's the output of the following code:

```
lst = [[c for c in range(r)] for r in range(3)]
for x in lst:
    for y in x:
        if y < 2:
            print('*', end=")
```

A. ***

B. **

C. *

    *

D. *

33) What's the output of the following code:

```
lst = [2 ** x for x in range(0, 11)]
print(lst[-1])
```

A. 1020

B. 1022

C. 1024

D. 1025

34) What's the output of the following code:

```
def fun(a, b=0, c=5, d=1):
    return a ** b ** c

print(fun(b=2, a=2, c=3))
```

A. 250

B. 255

C. 256

D. Syntax error

35) What's the output of the following code:

```
x = 5
f = lambda x: 1 + 2
print(f(x))
```

A. 0

B. 1

C. 2

D. 3

36) What's the output of the following code:

```
x = 1 # line 1
def a(x): # line 2
    return 2 * x
# line 3
x = 2 + a(x) # line 4
print(a(x)) # line 5
```

A. 0

B. 5

C. 8

D. 10

37) What's the output of the following code:

```
s = 'SPAM'
def f(x):
    return s + 'MAPS'
print(f(s))
```

A. SPAMMAPS

B. SPAM

C. MAPS

D. Syntax error

38) What's the output of the following code:

```
def gen():
    lst = range(5)
    for i in lst:
        yield i*i

for i in gen():
    print(i, end="")
```

A. 0

B. 014916

C. 619410

D. Syntax error

39) The output of the following expression is TRUE or FALSE

```
x = 0
try:
    print(x)
    print(1 / x)
except ZeroDivisionError:
    print("ERROR MESSAGE")
finally:
    print(x + 1)
print(x + 2)
```

Output:

0

ERROR MESSAGE

1

2

A. True

B. False

40) What's the output of the following code:

```
class A:
    def a(self):
        print("A", end='')
```

```
class B(A):
    def a(self):
        print("B", end=")

class C(B):
    def b(self):
        print("B", end=")

a = A()
b = B()
c = C()
a.a()
b.a()
c.b()
```

A. BBA

B. BBB

C. ABB

D. AAB

ANSWERS & EXPLANATION

1) Correct answer: D

The correct line to read 16 bytes from a binary file into a bytearray named data would be:

D. data = bytearray(binfile.read(16))

Option D is the most appropriate way to achieve the desired result. It reads 16 bytes from the binary file using the read method and then creates a bytearray from the read data.

2) Correct answer: AB

A. len("·) == 1 - This expression contains an empty string " followed by a bullet point character ('·'). The length of this string is 1 due to the bullet point character, so this expression is True.

B. len(""" """) == 0 - This expression contains a string with three space characters inside triple quotes. The length of this string is indeed 0, so this expression is True.

C. chr(ord("A") + 1) == 'B' - This expression takes the character 'A', converts it to its ASCII code (ord("A")), adds 1 to it, and then converts it back to a character using chr. The result of this expression is 'B', so it is True.

D. ord("Z") - ord("z") - ord("0") - This expression calculates the difference between the ASCII values of 'Z', 'z', and '0'. The ASCII value of 'Z' is greater than 'z', and 'z' is greater than '0', so the result is non-negative, meaning it's greater than or equal to 0. Therefore, this expression is True.

So, the two expressions that evaluate to True are:

A. len(".) == 1

B. len(""" """) == 0

3) Correct answer: CD

C. If open() 's second argument is 'r', the file must exist or open will fail.

This statement is true. When you open a file in 'r' mode (read mode), the file must exist; otherwise, the open operation will fail.

D. If open()'s second argument is 'w' and the invocation succeeds, the previous file's content is lost.

This statement is true. When you open a file in 'w' mode (write mode), it creates a new file or truncates the existing file, effectively erasing its previous content.

The other statements are not correct:

A. Closing an open file is performed by the close() function.

This statement is true. You close an open file in Python using the close() method, not closefile().

B. The second argument of the open() function describes the open mode and defaults to 'w'.

This statement is not true. The second argument of the open() function describes the open mode, but it defaults to 'r' (read mode) if not specified.

4) The correct answer is:

B. Instances of base classes (class objects)

In Python, the __bases__ property contains references to the base (parent) classes of a class, which are represented as class objects.

5) Correct answer: AC

A. Encapsulation allows you to control access to data and protect it from uncontrolled access. Encapsulation is one of the fundamental principles of OOP that helps hide the internal details of an object and restrict direct access to data.

C. Inheritance represents the relationship between a superclass and its subclass. Inheritance is a core concept in OOP where a subclass can inherit attributes and behaviors from a superclass.

Option B is not necessarily true. In class diagrams, arrows can indicate various relationships, including inheritance, association, or dependencies. The direction of the arrow can vary based on the specific relationship being represented.

Option D is not correct because it states that "an object is a recipe for a class," which is not accurate. An object is an instance of a class, and a class defines the blueprint or structure for creating objects.

6) Correct answer: CD

C) len("") == 2 - This option contains a string with two empty single quotes. The len() function correctly reports the length of the string, which is 2.

D) chr(ord('z') - 1) == 'Y' - This option correctly takes the character 'z', calculates its ASCII value using ord(), subtracts 1, and then converts the result back to a character using chr(). The result is 'Y'.

7) Correct answer: AC

A. If an exception occurs when invoking open(), an exception is raised. - When there is an issue with opening a file, Python will raise an exception, such as a FileNotFoundError, if the file cannot be found.

C. The open() function returns an object representing a physical file. - The open() function returns a file object that represents a physical file on the file system, allowing you to interact with it.

Option B is not always true. While it's common to provide a second argument that specifies the file's open mode (e.g., 'r' for reading or 'w' for writing), it's not always required. If you don't provide the second argument, 'r' (read mode) is used by default.

Option D refers to standard input (stdin), standard output (stdout), and standard error (stderr) streams, but it's not directly related to the open() function.

8) Correct answer: BC

B. a != b

C. a is not None

9) Correct answer: AD

```
1    class A:
2        pass
3    class B(A):
4        pass
5    class C(A):
6        pass
7    class D(B):
8        pass
9
10   class Class_4(D, A):
11       pass
12   class Class_3(A, C):
13       pass
14   class Class_2(B, D):
15       pass
16
17   class Class_1(C, D):
18       pass
19
```

Can't be B, class A shouldn't be before class C, because class C is a subclass of class A.

Reference:

https://www.datacamp.com/community/tutorials/super-multiple-inheritance-diamond-problem

10) Correct answer: D

```
 8  my_list = [i for i in range (5, 0, -1)]
 9  m = [my_list[i] for i in range (5) ] if my_list[i] % 2 == 0]
10  print(m)
11
```

```
                                                              input
 File "main.py", line 9
   m = [my_list[i] for i in range (5) ] if my_list[i] % 2 == 0]
                                       ^
SyntaxError: unmatched ']'
```

Answer is indeed D, due to the] before the if statement.

If this bracket wouldnt be there, the result would be [4, 2].

my_list = [i for i in range(5,0,-1)]

m = [my_list[i] for i in range(5) if my_list[i] % 2 == 0]

print(m)

[4, 2]

if] in the correct place, then the correct answer would be A

12) Correct answer: AB

The correct options to correctly call the pyfun() function from the Python module named pymod are:

Option A: from pymod import pyfun

This snippet correctly imports the pyfun function from the pymod module, allowing you to invoke it as pyfun().

Option B: import pymod

With this import statement, you can invoke the function using pymod.pyfun(). For example: pymod.pyfun().

Options C and D contain incorrect syntax or misplaced function calls.

12) Correct answer: AB

Among the provided invocations in Python, the following two are valid:

A. sorted("python") - This is a valid invocation of the sorted() function to sort the characters in the string "python."

B. "python".sort() - This is not a valid invocation. The sort() method is not available for strings. You should use sorted("python") to sort a string.

Options C and D contain incorrect syntax and are not valid invocations.

13) Correct answer: C

```
 4 ▾ class Class:
 5       Variable = 0
 6 ▾    def __init__(self):
 7           self.value = 0
 8
 9   object_1 = Class()
10   Class.Variable += 1
11   object_2 = Class()
12   object_2.value += 1
13   print(object_2.Variable + object_1.value)
14
```

Ln: 12, Col: 10

▶ Run   ↪ Share   Command Line Arguments

1

14) Correct answer: D

try:

   f = open("linije","w")

   print(1, end="")

   s = f.readline()

   print(2, end="")

except IOError as error:

   print(3, end="")

else:

    f.close()

    print(4,end="")

15) Correct answer: AB

A. math.hypot(3, 4) == math.sqrt(25) - This expression calculates the Euclidean norm (hypotenuse) of a right triangle with legs of length 3 and 4. It correctly checks if the hypotenuse is equal to the square root of 25, which is True.

B. math.hypot(2, 5) == math.trunc(2.5) - This expression calculates the Euclidean norm of a right triangle with legs of length 2 and 5. It correctly checks if the hypotenuse is equal to the truncated value of 2.5, which is also True.

Options C and D contain incorrect function names and syntax and would not evaluate to True.

16) Correct answer: CD

C. The constructor in Python is a method named init. - In Python, the constructor is a special method named __init__, which is automatically called when an object of the class is created.

D. The constructor must have at least one parameter. - While it's common to define the constructor with the self-parameter, which refers to the instance itself, the constructor can have other parameters as well. However, it's not strictly required to have additional parameters besides self.

17) Correct answer: D

The function foo takes two arguments, x and y. x is just a regular variable, while y is a function that takes one argument.

In the body of the function, y(x) is the first function call. This calls the function y with x as its argument. In the example code, y is a lambda function that squares its argument, so y(x) computes the square of x.

The second function call is y(x+1). This calls the same y function, but with x+1 as its argument. In the example code, this computes the square of x+1.

Finally, the two results from the function calls are added together, and the sum is returned by foo.

In the example code, foo(1, lambda x: x*x) is called. This passes 1 as the value of x and a lambda function that squares its argument as the value of y. Therefore, y(x) evaluates to 1 squared, which is 1, and y(x+1) evaluates to 2 squared, which is 4. The sum of these two values is 5, which is the value returned by foo.

```
1  import sys
2
3  b1 = type (dir(sys)) is str
4  b2 = type(sys.path[-1]) is str
5  print(b1 and b2)
```

STDIN

Input for
Optional

Output:

False

18) Correct answer: A

The provided code contains a few syntax errors, including missing parentheses and a misplaced closing brace. Here's the corrected code and its expected output:

def foo(x, y, z):

    return x(y) - x(z)

```
print(foo(lambda x: x % 2, 2, 1))
```

With the corrected code, the expected output is:

A. 1

The code defines a function foo that takes three arguments and applies a function x to y and z, subtracting the results. In the print statement, it calls foo with a lambda function that calculates the modulo 2 of its argument. When you pass 2 and 1 as y and z, respectively, you get 1 % 2 - 2 % 2, which is 1 - 0, resulting in 1.

19) Correct answer: C

The provided code contains two print statements that each output a string. Here's the expected output of each print statement:

print("Peter's sister's name's \"Anna\"") - This statement prints the following string:

Peter's sister's name's "Anna"

print('Peter\'s sister\'s name\'s "Anna"') - This statement prints the following string:

Peter's sister's name's "Anna"

Both statements correctly handle escaping single quotes and double quotes to print the intended string. The output of both print statements is the same as shown above.

20) Correct answer: B

The output of the given code is:

B. 125

Here's how the code works:

The initial value of i is set to 250.

The while loop checks the length of the string representation of i, and as long as it's greater than 72, it multiplies i by 2.

In the else block, it divides i by 2 (which effectively undoes the last multiplication operation).

The final value of i is 125, so it prints 125 as the output.

21) Correct answer: A

This code uses a while loop to increment the value of 'n' until it reaches 4. It then prints the value of 'n' at each iteration. The output would be:

1 2 3 4

22) Correct answer: A

Let's break down the code.

x is initially assigned the value 0.

y is assigned the value 2.

z is assigned the length of the string "Python", which is 6 characters.

x is then assigned the result of the comparison y > z, which evaluates to False since 2 is not greater than 6.

Thus, the output will be:

False

<class 'bool'>

The type(x) function call returns the data type of x, which in this case is a boolean (<class 'bool'>).

23) Correct answer: A

This code performs a swap of values between two variables (Val and Val2) without using a temporary variable. It uses the XOR bitwise operation. Let's break it down step by step:

Val = Val ^ Val2: This XOR operation swaps the values of Val and Val2.

Val2 = Val ^ Val2: This line swaps the values back to their original state using XOR operation with the updated Val and the original Val2.

Val = Val ^ Val2: This XOR operation again swaps the values, making Val hold the original value of Val2.

So, after these operations, Val will contain the original value of Val2, which is 0. Hence, the output will be 0.

24) Correct answer: C

The code provided in the snippet:

z, y, x = 2, 1, 0

x, z = z, y

y = y - z

x, y, z = y, z, x

print(x, y, z)

When executed, results in the output:

0 1 2

Therefore, the correct option is C. 0 1 2.

25) Correct answer: D

Let's break down the code step by step:

a = 0: Sets the variable a to 0.

b = a ** 0: Any number raised to the power of 0 is 1. Therefore, b is assigned the value 1.

if b < a + 1: As b is 1 and a + 1 is 1, the condition is false. It moves to the elif statement.

elif b == 1: This condition is true since b is indeed 1. It assigns c = 2.

print(a + b + c): Adds a (0), b (1), and c (2) together.

The output will be 3.

26) Correct answer: A

This code initiates a while loop that decrements the value of i by 3 in each iteration until i becomes less than or equal to 3. Upon each iteration, it prints a single "*". Once i becomes 3 or less, the loop is broken.

In this case, the loop breaks when i becomes 1, as subtracting 3 from 1 would make i -2, which is not greater than 3. Then, the else block doesn't get executed as the loop terminates without reaching its completion.

Therefore, the output will be a series of asterisks () printed on separate lines, without the final "" from the else block:

*

*

*

27) Correct answer: A

The code you provided prints the asterisk (*) using a for loop that iterates over the range from 1 to 4 with a step of 2 (range(1, 4, 2)).

This loop will execute twice and print an asterisk each time. After the loop, it won't print anything else.

The output is indeed:

*

*

So, the correct answer is A. True.

28) Correct answer: A

When you compare two strings in Python using the > operator, it compares them lexicographically, i.e., it checks their Unicode code point values character by character.

In this case, you're comparing the strings "20" and "30".

The comparison starts with the first character of each string. In this scenario, "3" from the string "30" has a greater Unicode code point than "2" from the string "20". Therefore, "30" is considered greater than "20".

So, print(x > y) will output False.

29) Correct answer: B

The code utilizes the del statement to delete elements from the list lst using list slicing.

del lst[0:-2] deletes elements from index 0 up to the element at the second-to-last index (i.e., -2 specifies the second-to-last element, which is "C").

Initially, the list is ["A", "B", "C", 2, 4]. Removing elements from 0 to the second-to-last element would result in the list retaining the elements starting from the second-to-last index and beyond.

Therefore, the output will be:

[2, 4]

So, the correct option is B. [2, 4].

30) Correct answer: C

The code iterates over the keys of the dictionary and prints each key in a separate line using the loop for item in dict:.

The output will be:

a

b

c

So, the correct option is C

31) Correct answer: B

The code provided iterates through each character in the string s, converts the character to uppercase, and assigns it to the variable i. However, this change in i doesn't modify the original string s. Strings in Python are immutable, so altering i doesn't affect the content of s.

The print(s, end="") statement prints the original string s after the loop has executed, ensuring the content of s remains unchanged.

Therefore, the output will be the original string:

python

So, the correct answer is B. python.

32) Correct answer: A

Let's break down the code:

The code creates a list of lists (lst) using list comprehensions. It generates lists of numbers from 0 up to the specified range in each inner list, where the outer list comprehension iterates over the range from 0 to 2 ([0, 1, 2]) and the inner list comprehension generates the list based on the current value of the outer loop. So, lst becomes [[0], [0, 1], [0, 1, 2]].

The nested loops then iterate through each element in the lists within lst. For each element (y) in the inner lists, it checks if the element is less than 2. If true, it prints an asterisk ('*').

The output will be all the asterisks printed:

***

Therefore, the correct answer is A. ***.

33) Correct answer: C

The code creates a list lst using a list comprehension that calculates 2 raised to the power of x for x ranging from 0 to 10. The expression 2 ** x computes powers of 2.

Therefore, lst will contain powers of 2: [1, 2, 4, 8, 16, 32, 64, 128, 256, 512, 1024].

The line print(lst[-1]) prints the last element of the list, which is 1024.

So, the correct answer is C. 1024.

34) Correct answer: C

The function fun takes four parameters (a, b, c, and d) and performs a series of exponentiations: a ** (b ** c).

When the function fun is called with fun(b=2, a=2, c=3), it computes 2 ** (2 ** 3). First, it calculates the exponentiation 2 ** 3 which results in 8, then it computes 2 ** 8, resulting in 256.

Therefore, the output of the code will be:

256

Hence, the correct answer is C. 256.

35) Correct answer: D

The provided code defines a lambda function f that takes an argument x but doesn't use it. Instead, it returns the value 1 + 2.

When f(x) is called with x = 5, the lambda function ignores the passed value of x and always returns 1 + 2, which is 3.

Thus, the output of the code will be:

3

Hence, the correct answer is D. 3.

36) Correct answer: C

Let's break down the code step by step:

x = 1: Sets the variable x to 1.

def a(x):: Defines a function a that takes a parameter x.

return 2 * x: The function a simply returns double the value of x.

x = 2 + a(x): Updates the value of x by adding 2 to the result of the function a(x) where x is currently 1. So, a(1) will return 2 * 1 = 2, and x becomes 2 + 2 = 4.

print(a(x)): Calls the function a with the updated value of x (which is 4). a(4) will return 2 * 4 = 8, and this result is printed.

The output of the code will be:

8

So, the correct answer is C. 8.

37) Correct answer: A

The code defines a function f(x) that takes an argument x and returns the concatenation of the global variable s ('SPAM') with the string 'MAPS'.

When f(s) is called, it passes the string 'SPAM' as an argument to the function f. Inside the function, it appends 'MAPS' to 'SPAM' and returns the result.

The output of the code will be:

SPAMMAPS

Therefore, the correct answer is A. SPAMMAPS.

38) Correct answer: B

The code defines a generator function gen() that yields the square of each number in the range from 0 to 4.

When iterating through the generator by using a for loop for i in gen():, it prints each yielded value with end="", meaning there won't be any spaces or new lines between the printed values.

The output of the code will be the squares of numbers 0 to 4 printed without separation:

014916

Hence, the correct answer is B. 014916.

39) Correct answer: A

The provided code utilizes a try-except block to manage a potential ZeroDivisionError. It prints '0', catches the ZeroDivisionError due to the division by zero (1 / x), and prints an error message 'ERROR MESSAGE'. It then executes the finally block regardless of whether an exception occurred, printing x + 1, where x = 0. Finally, it attempts to print x + 2.

The code will execute without throwing an unhandled exception since the error is caught by the except block. The output will be:

0

ERROR MESSAGE

1

2

40) Correct answer: C

The code defines three classes: A, B (inheriting from A), and C (inheriting from B). Class A has a method a(), and both classes B and C have a method a() and b() respectively.

Instance a is an object of class A.

Instance b is an object of class B.

Instance c is an object of class C.

When the methods are called on these instances, they execute the corresponding methods defined in their classes.

a.a(): Calls method a() of class A. It prints "A" without a newline.

b.a(): Calls method a() of class B. It prints "B" without a newline.

c.b(): Calls method b() of class C. It prints "B" without a newline.

The output will be:

ABB

Hence, the correct answer is C. ABB.

End of Practice Test III

Notes:

GEORGIODACCACHE

....
....
....
....
....
....
....

GOOD LUCK!

www.ingramcontent.com/pod-product-compliance
Lightning Source LLC
LaVergne TN
LVHW051655050326
832903LV00032B/3834